Don't Call Me Mum!

A play by Julia Donaldson

Illustrated by Julia Patton

Characters

Mrs W
(Mrs Wilson)

Josh

Amit

Erin Oscar Maddie

At home

Mrs W: Time to go, Josh.

Josh: Okay, Mum.

Mrs W: Don't call me Mum at school, okay?

Josh: But you are my mum.

Mrs W: Yes, but at school you must call me Mrs Wilson. You keep forgetting!

Mrs. Wilson

At school

Mrs W: Good morning, children. I'd like you to write about what you did on the weekend.

Erin: Mrs Wilson!

Mrs W: Yes, Erin?

Erin: I can't remember what I did.

Mrs W: Then think!

Maddie: Mrs Wilson!

Mrs W: Yes, Maddie?

Maddie: My pencil is blunt.

Mrs W: Then sharpen it!

Amit: Mrs Wilson! Oscar took my rubber.

Oscar: I did not!

Josh: Mum!

Mrs W: Don't call me Mum. What is it?

Josh: Can I have a sandwich?

Mrs W: No! Now, it's time to hear what you have written. Let's take turns, starting with Oscar.

Oscar: Yes, Mrs Wilson. "On the weekend I went to a soccer match."

Erin: "On the weekend I rode my bike."

Maddie: "On the weekend I went to my Gran's."

Amit: "On the weekend I cut my finger."

Mrs W: Oh dear. Is it better now?

Amit: Yes, Mrs Wilson.

Mrs W: Good. Now, Josh, what have you written?

Josh: Nothing, Mum.

Oscar: Don't call her Mum!

Maddie: She's Mrs Wilson!

Mrs W: Why have you written nothing?

Josh: Well, you know what we did on the weekend.

Mrs W: Yes, but you have to pretend I don't know.

Josh: Sorry, Mum.

Amit: DON'T CALL HER MUM!

In the lunch room

Oscar: Mrs Wilson! Amit took my apple.

Amit: I did not!

Erin: Mrs Wilson! My drink has spilt.

Mrs W: Here is a cloth.

Maddie: Mrs Wilson! Josh keeps moaning!

Mrs W: What is it, Josh?

Josh: There are no lollies in my lunch box, Mum.

Mrs W: Don't call me Mum.

Erin: She's Mrs Wilson.

Oscar: And we're not allowed to have lollies.

Josh: That's a silly rule, Mum.

Mrs W: DON'T CALL ME MUM!

Mrs Wilson

Back at home.

Mrs W: Well, Josh, did you enjoy school today?

Josh: Yes thanks, Mrs Wilson.